# 21st Century Relationships

## BOOK TWO

## WHY HUMANS WEREN'T DESIGNED FOR MARRIAGE

*CARLA SAVANNAH*

# Contents

# Acknowledgements

*"To all the men I've loved before. Who travelled in and out my door."* (Music please – Julio Iglesias and Willy Nelson) Nah, just kidding, I haven't loved that many.

This book really is a culmination of everything I've learnt in all of my relationships and interactions in the dating scene. These experiences have helped me learn so much about others, and most importantly myself. Over time I've had the privilege of experiencing some of the most painful and most fruitful relationships. I have to thank every soul that has entered my life because I took a small lesson from each of them.

While my personal experiences have given me wisdom, I've also gained a lot of knowledge through my relationship counsellor work. I want to take my hat off to every relationship counsellor out there; it is a very challenging field to work in! There's no one-size-fits-all in relationships. Each is so different and unique. What works in some may not work in others.

As a relationship counsellor, you have to be ready to adapt quickly, remain open-minded, and have a solid understanding of your own biases. It's not an easy job to get everyone on the same page.

Counsellors are only human; we have our relationship challenges too. During those times, our job requires us to be kind to ourselves and make sure we have the right support to remain strong for the people we help. Supporting others while also supporting the self can sometimes be challenging, but it's what makes us all blood and bone.

I hope this book serves you all well.

# CHAPTER 1

## An Introduction

Hopefully, you have read my previous book, *21st Century Relationships*. If you haven't, I highly recommend you start there first. If you decide to jump right into book two, I can guarantee that it will be just as informative and will give you some great tools.

If you have read *21st Century Relationships*, you will find that I greatly expand on previously discussed areas. You will have a pretty good idea of my writing style, and you will know that I take a blunt, no BS approach with my writing. Before we get started, I want to offer a brief warning. If you're highly sensitive, I'm not the right writer for you. My books are not for you if you're not inclined whatsoever toward esoteric concepts and spiritual beliefs. If you have strong personal or religious beliefs around the need for marriage, this book will challenge you to look at another perspective.

However, if you remain open-minded enough, you may look at the ritualistic contract of marriage with new eyes and possibly even manage to improve your marriage. That's if you don't choose to throw your partner over a balcony first. (I'm just kidding!)

This book will address old fashioned as well as modern ideas around marriage. It will explore the positive aspects of the concept and ritual of marriage and dig deeper into the elements that have been seriously misconstrued by the human need to feel safe and secure.

This book will also touch upon some information indicating that being married wasn't how humans were intended to live. On the opposite side of the spectrum, I will also address some unrealistic New Age, spiritual, and utopian concepts.

Ultimately this book is intended to open your mind and question whether you genuinely think marriage, the way we understand it today, is necessary.

Enjoy the read!

## CHAPTER 2

# Runaway bride

As a typical young girl in the 80s, I had heard stories like Sleeping Beauty and Snow White a million times. I was led to believe that a Prince would come along and sweep me off my feet. We would marry and live happily ever after. Like many other little girls, I dreamed of my wedding day and having children of my own. And that was the extent of my thinking about my future. Nothing else happens after that, right?

In my rush to reach my happily ever after, I got engaged when I was just 16. That relationship didn't work out. I almost got engaged again at 20 to a different boy but concluded that he wasn't my Prince Charming either and moved on. Engagement number three happened when I was 24, and again, things didn't work out. The closer I got to being married, the more afraid I became, and I would run. I was Julia Roberts from the movie Runaway Bride.

Growing up, all I ever heard from my mother was, "MEN are all selfish, I've had nothing but terrible relationships. I only attract shit men!" My Mother believed she was always the victim in her relationships.

When I think back over my life, I was the complete opposite of my mother. I was very lucky with Men I think. I seemed to attract nice guys, thankfully! In fact, I'd often feel sorry for *them* and most of the time believed that they all deserved much better than me. I now know that these were just insecurities placed upon me by my Mother.

I remember once my Mother telling me the story about my Grandparents. Apparently, my grandfather would often cheat and come home late to my grandmother. My grandfather had the audacity to one day come home late and as he got into bed with my grandmother he said to her "Why don't you ever ask me where I have been?" to which my grandmother replied "Because I don't want to know as I fear it will break my heart."

What an incredibly strong woman. She knew what he was doing but she didn't want the confirmation. Immediately I thought though, relationships are full of falsehoods and lies. I thought, being an adult means you can never be truthful again because saying the truth carries too many consequences with it. That was the beginning of my conditioning around what marriage is.

Interestingly, for some reason, I can't wear rings on my wedding finger. I get terrible allergies to metals, particularly on that finger. If I manage to wear a ring, I have to remove it after a few hours and am usually left with a band of eczema. I always found this peculiar until I visited a well-known medium. She asked me, "*Why are the spirits constantly trying to take the wedding ring off your finger? They keep sabotaging your relationships. It appears there is a curse placed on all the women in your family.*" She told me that my grandfather had an affair with a witch in Portugal. This witch cursed my grandmother and the women in my family to never be happy in a relationship. Initially, I didn't believe the medium, but my mind changed after asking some family members who confirmed the story about my grandfather and his witch mistress.

I must admit, after hearing this information, I resigned to the thought that I would be single forever. I joked that the only way I'd make it down the aisle would be if I get married almost immediately after getting engaged. The quicker it happened, the less time I'd have to think about it and get cold feet. And that's how it happened.

I met my now-husband in Portugal and fell so madly in love that I would have given up almost anything to be with him. I say almost anything because my daughter was my biggest priority at the time. She was one person I wasn't willing to turn my back on. So, while I would have loved to move to Portugal, I couldn't leave her behind in Australia.

Carlos and I wanted to be together so badly that we had to rush the process and get married so he could move to Australia to live with my daughter and me. Carlos came to Australia, and we were married within a few months. We hadn't even known each other more than nine months before we married. We have learnt more about each other within marriage than we ever knew before the big commitment. The rush worked because I honestly thought I'd never make it down the aisle. I'll be honest I did lose my breath and choke a little when I was about to say the Vows. Not because I didn't love him, but because all my ancestral fears hit me all at once.

So, our reason for marriage was an overwhelming desire to be together and needing to bridge the geographical distance between us. Yes, it happened very quickly, but I don't regret my decision. I've learnt and grown with

Carlos. Even if we were ever to go our separate ways in the future, I'd never regret a moment because the experience of being married to Carlos has made me a better person.

However, if you were to ask me whether I would ever marry another or again, I would probably say I don't think so, simply because I see no necessity for it.

Some important questions you should ask yourself are:

- What are your reasons for wanting to marry?
- Is it because you have a dream or fantasy in your mind about how marriage will be?
- Is it because you are lonely?
- Is it because you want someone to take care of you?
- Is it because you want to take care of someone?

- Is it because you've been taught by culture or religion that it's necessary?

- Is it because you believe that someone else will meet your needs and that you are incomplete without someone else in your life?

- Is it because you think you shouldn't have kids before marriage?

- Do you just want a special day of celebration where you can dress up like a princess and look and feel like royalty.

I want you to take a moment to really think about this. Jot down some reasons why you want to get married? What expectations do you have of your marriage? What do you believe will happen once you are married?

There's no right or wrong here! It's your personal feelings and beliefs. You need to be honest with yourself. Spend some time answering these questions before moving on to the next chapter.

CHAPTER 3

# We came from oneness into separation

You started as an idea, an inspiration from the larger

consciousness field. You are the result, expression and

outcome of an idea put forward from Source Energy, God

if you will. You are the consequence of God's imagination.


You were created in the mind first, and it's the mind and

consciousness that moved matter into what you are today.

*(If you want an excellent documentary to watch that illustrates how*

*science is now confirming this, watch Superhuman: The Invisible*

*Made Visible.*)


Let's start with the basics. Physically, you started as one cell. That cell was exposed to specific laws associated with pressure, heat and vibration. It divided into two, then four and so on. Each cell in your body has an individual consciousness doing its job. It groups up with other like-minded cells to create organs. Each organ is a collection of those conscious cells. Your whole body is made up of organs; therefore, your body is made up of many groups of consciousness working as one big collective consciousness. You are a consciousness, within a consciousness within a larger consciousness system. That is this body that you are today. Your whole body is seen as God to one tiny cell in your intestine.

Now let's look at it from a spiritual perspective. You are a small drop of energy from the original collective Source of energy. You are an individual unit of consciousness from the collective consciousness. You are an individual Soul that is part of the original One soul that it extended out from.

To expand on this idea, a family, community, country, and planet comprises a collection of consciousness working together, one within the other, not separate from each other. What your planet does affects you as a country. What your country does affects your community. What your community does affects your family, and what your family does affects YOU! In this way, you are not separate from your world. There's a common energy and vibration that permeates through all things. Do you understand how your micro world works within your macro world? How they are all related and not separate? They all are a part of each other, one within the other.

Can you understand how thinking that you are energetically separate from the Source of all that is, is so unfathomable? You may perceive physical separation; however, energetically wise, you are one inside of the other. A cell inside your body is merely a separate individual cell inside your body; it is not separate from your body. That cell makes up who you are.

With this knowledge, let's move on to an even bigger perspective. When you are functioning as a collective consciousness in Oneness of Energy, you have less free will because you are subject to the decisions of a collective.

However, when you are functioning as an individual cell or unit of consciousness, there is a sense of separation. Therefore, you have more free will as a physical being.

Let's put this in practical terms. Imagine that you are part of a family. To function well as a family, you need to consider teamwork and the whole family's needs—the collective. As a result, you may not have as much freedom to choose what to eat, watch, or do because you need to consider others within the family. We experience less free will within a collective of beings.

However, when you are on your own, you can choose what to eat, watch and do because you aren't stepping on another person's toes with your personal decisions. You have a greater degree of free will.

Sometimes I say to people, to help your body heal, you need to address the individual cells in your body first and program them. You then move onto the collective of cells related to that area of your body, be it an organ or a system of cells. The next step is programming the whole body together. You're working your way from the micro to the macro.

You may be wondering what all this has to do with the topic of this book. Well, everything! When you see yourself as a separate individual, you have lots of free will. When you see yourself as a part of a collective, your free will also depends on other people's free will.

The one major universal law that any energy or entity must acknowledge its free will. There's a reason why a bouncing ball doesn't go through the ground. There's a reason why you don't become enmeshed as one when you hug someone. In dense physical reality, freedom is a given. You don't go back to being one cell again in your mother's womb, ever.

In the world of physicality, you can make choices as an individual. In the world of energy or spirituality, the more outward you expand toward more dimensions, energy makes choices as a collective, resulting in less free will.

Now remember you moved towards density, down the dimensions, here to physical 3D Earth, as an individual consciousness to experience yourself as a separate individual. That was the choice you made. Your soul chose to explore Earth. Your soul chose to incarnate in human form and experience the consequences of individuality. You would never have incarnated here if you didn't want to experience what it was like to be separate from your Source.

The soul's journey reminds me of the Prodigal Son, leaving home to go on an adventure. The Prodigal Son goes out to grow, have time to self-reflect and get to know himself better, only to eventually return with the knowledge of all its adventures and experiences. The Prodigal Son, while part of the family, doesn't understand or appreciate what he has. Only when he is separated can he truly understand what he was once a part of. You have to feel total separation first before you can appreciate the comfort of togetherness. Herein lies the purpose of your physical existence.

The experience of the Prodigal Son is reflected in our human journey. You didn't know any different when you left Source to come here to explore. You were once part of a powerful collective but have now experienced separation. As a result of this experience, you can appreciate what you once had. It may even inspire you to create a collective consciousness of your own. You are God experiencing itself in physical form. You are God learning about itself, interacting with itself, expanding itself through you!

Knowing that you chose to come down to Earth, to experience separation and free will and your surroundings physically, would it make sense for your physical human self to now tell your exploring Soul, that you have to be constrained to only one country, one job, one relationship, one experience for the rest of your life? You chose to come here to experience freedom, yet you get here, and your physical body (the ego-self) tries to convince you that you are not free! How absurd is that?

If free will is the ultimate decision we make, then traditional views of marriage no longer make sense.

# CHAPTER 4

## *A relationship starts with the desire to go home*

When you separated from Source, the one original Energy, it created a sense of confusion within you. It would have felt just as confusing as being expelled from your mother's uterus. You were safe, warm, and protected, part of a system. There was structure and order to things. Then suddenly, you were ejected out into a cold world. You had to learn how to operate the physical vehicle your Soul was now animating.

The emotions that arise from being separated from your original Source of Energy and life force are the same as separating from your mother's womb. These emotions are what I call your Soul wounds. The most common Soul wounds are confusion, abandonment, disconnection, rejection, unacceptance, powerlessness, detachment.

These wounds manifest into feelings of being unloved and unwanted. These are the first emotions that were triggered within your Soul due to your separation from Source or your mother. We spend lifetimes trying to resolve these emotions until we eventually are confronted with the truth.

You then spend years and sometimes lifetimes desperately searching to feel whole again. You spend years in a physical body seeking belonging, acceptance, safety, security, unconditional love and connection again. You seek this from your parents, and when that doesn't work, you seek it through friendships. When friendships aren't fruitful, you seek out these emotions through partners or communities. If that doesn't work, you may decide that home doesn't exist, and you give up.

Sadly, some think it's not possible ever to find this unconditional love and peace again. Some even take their own life trying to find it, only to feel even more alone. They discover that it wasn't something given to them; it's what they originally were part of from the beginning, so they never lost that energetic connection. If you didn't give up, you realise that no one else and nothing external can give you that; you seek these emotions or feelings within yourself.

A relationship starts with the desire to go home. That is what you are longing for when you seek out relationships. You are longing for that feeling of home that you once felt when you were a part of everything - when you were one with Source when you were one with your mother. You felt no separation; you were connected, safe, accepted and loved. You belonged somewhere, and you were a part of something.

A relationship can end just as quickly over the fear of not having your emotional wounds resolved. When you notice that your partner can't give you all the unconditional love, acceptance, belonging and connection that you once had, you may seek out more partners in a desperate attempt to re-establish feelings lost upon your separation from your Source.

Most of the time, relationships end due to the fear of not getting those feelings back, the feelings of "I'm never going back home to unconditional love." Placing the responsibility of re-establishing wholeness onto another person is simply an unrealistic expectation of this physical 3D world, where there is so much separation.

By now, you must be thinking, is it even possible to feel whole, to ever feel home and connected again? The answer is yes! However, seeking this wholeness from another person in the same pursuit of happiness is not the answer. How can someone give you what they don't have? The sense of completion, home and connection come from within you. This realisation inspired the creation of my own modality of healing called 8 Selves Therapy. But more on that later. First, we need to explore the topic of inner selves.

CHAPTER 5

# Reconciling the inner selves

I'm sure you're aware by now that there may be various dialogues going on in your head. Some people call it the little angel and the little devil on each shoulder. Some call it the ego and the Higher Self. Either way, most of us experience internal dialogue at some point in our lives.

There are so many mind games that can influence decisions when these different parts of the self get involved. Say, for example, that one part of you says, "We should start a business!". Then another part chimes in with, "I don't know how to do that. How will I get clients? Who would want to pay me for what I have to offer? What if I fail and look bad?" Things can get a little confusing.

The different parts of the self often have entirely different biases. Each prefers different situations, environments and states of being. Interestingly, they tend to either blame each other or place the responsibility on each other. They rely on the other to fulfil their needs, or they can become selfish and demand that their own needs be met. Does this sound familiar? Isn't this the battle you regularly experience in your daily friendships and relationships? One friend says, "I want chocolate cake!" And the other states, "But you'll get fat!". It's the same battle that goes on within your mind every day, between you and another version of you. How can you expect to make amends and create deep connections with another human when you can't bring together the two selves that are having it out in your mind? You can't even get You and You on the same page.

How do you deal with an inner monologue that belittles you, saying, "You idiot! Why did you do that?" Do you surrender and say, "Yes, I am an idiot"? Do you get upset and retaliate? Do you go into victim mode? Pay close attention to the way you deal with the internal conflict within yourself. In Psychology, this is called Cognitive Dissonance. It occurs when a person holds contradictory beliefs, ideas, or values and is typically experienced as psychological stress when they participate in an action against one or more of their inner selves.

The challenge is to get them on the same page, getting them to work together. When one says, "You idiot, why did you do that?" the other should respond with, "No! We are in this together. We did it together. You are not alone in this, and I didn't act alone. If I take the blame, we are both to blame because we are one, and we are a team."

This battle often takes place in the 4th-dimensional realm, in the realm of emotions. The 4D is the middle ground and meeting point between our physical 3D world and our 5D world of energy and collective information. 4D is where emotions and thought-forms battle it out. I touch upon this topic in my book *Evolve Your Emotions, Evolve Through the Dimensions*, so I won't go into too much detail on this here.

Eventually, instead of there being conflict amongst your selves, there is co-operation within your selves. One can then comfort the other and provide support, unconditional love, and acceptance.

No matter how light or how dark the thoughts are that arise. When there is no longer internal conflict, a person can feel complete and whole again. You feel safer knowing that *you* will never leave *you*.

The therapy that I created, *8 Selves Therapy*, has the sole purpose of teaching people how to unlock hidden parts of themselves to eliminate this internal conflict between the different aspects of self—ultimately leading people towards what Psychologists term self-actualisation or self-realisation.

Getting all the selves working in unison helps create higher levels of conscious awareness. You then become a power to be reckoned with. When all selves are working together towards one common goal, you become unstoppable and manifesting your heart's desire is a breeze.

A person who feels whole and complete within does not seek to feel completed by another person. They are acting as a part of an internal team member. They can then take full responsibility for all aspects of themselves.

In my opinion, this is what humanity is struggling with at the moment. The spiritual community can accidentally become too focused on listening to their higher selves or higher minds only. Most materialists are too focused on listening solely to their physical needs and the basic primal survival senses. They wonder why an aspect of themselves isn't functioning to its fullest potential. The answer is, of course, that it is being ignored or suppressed.

Humanity needs to be focusing more on trying to bring various aspects of themselves together. How can we find more ways to get our higher self to acknowledge our physical needs? How can we find ways to express our physical needs without hurting and corrupting the lessons needed for our higher self to evolve? How can we provide opportunities for our soul to feel more freedom while allowing our physical body more opportunities to express itself creatively?

Remember, if the voice in your mind is you, then who is the one listening to it?

CHAPTER 6

# 8 Selves Therapy

We all came from the original Source; therefore, we carry all the qualities of the Source. I believe that we have eight parts to our Soul or 8 Selves that put together in essence, make up the totality of who we are.

The best way I can explain it is by using a cake analogy. Imagine that the one original Source of all is a cake. We need flour, eggs, milk, sugar, butter, etc. These are individual ingredients, but they create a delicious cake when mixed in the correct measurements. 8 Selves Therapy attempts to put all these ingredients of Source Energy together to make up an individual's Soul.

The 8 Selves we have within us are, in this very specific order:

1. The Survivalist Self

2. The Creative Self

3. The Boss Self

4. The Lover Self

5. The Student Self

6. The Teacher Self

7. The Liberated Self

8. The Wise Self

Let's take a look at them one by one.

## 1. The Survivalist Self

The Survivalist within is the part of you that is solely worried about your physical survival - your safety and security. It will worry about your physical health, having enough money, whether the doors are locked and whether you have enough food in your cupboard. This part of you is also concerned about how you fit into the world - whether you will be left alone to die or whether you will be cared for. It desires to be supported and told that nothing is wrong with them and their physical needs. This part of you wants to connect with like-minded people and find a sense of belonging somewhere for the sake of physical survival. When the Survivalist finally feels a sense of safety, security, and support, it can then communicate with the next Self.

## 2. The Creative Self

Lights! Camera! Action! The Creative within is adventurous or an action taker and is constantly doing. It's creating, producing, building, constructing and inventing. It creates simply for the sake of creating. For now, there is no purpose to their creation. A person with this Self fully activated looks like a little child eagerly playing with building blocks, constantly knocking their creations down to start anew. There's no real goal around this creativity. It's just merely creating for the sake of creating. It will look very busy and chaotic to the outside person observing them. They want what they want and will do what it takes to create it. After lots and lots of experimenting with their creativity and creations, they move on to the next Self.

## 3. The Boss Self

The Boss within us is the assertive, controlling, confident, organised and structured part of ourselves. The perfectionist within wants everything done just right and in order. Here a person is starting to create some rules within the game of their life. This part of the Self is very goal-driven. It wants to move towards its goals and create order and structure from the chaotic mess it made when acting as the previous Self. The Boss self thinks, "Well, I've manifested all of this now. How can I use what I have manifested to make what I want? What is the formula I can use to help me bring in more of what I want into my life?" Here the Self starts to get a sense of control over their world and themselves. Once this part of the Self feels as though it's now in control of itself, its survival, its creations, and its goals, it starts to direct its energy outward toward others. When this Self is activated, one begins to discover their role within society and understands what they offer. Here is where a career desire is birthed.

## 4. The Lover Self

This part of the Self desires to love and connect with others and feel loved and connected with themselves. The Lover is all about relationships and peaceful interactions, be it with others, themselves or their environment. The Lover is also the part of ourselves that desires to feel at a deeper level, not just at a physical level. It is highly connected to emotions and the desire to feel more. When the Lover self is activated, a person becomes more cooperative with others and society, takes responsibility for their actions, and desires to give and receive. Win/win interactions are more achievable, as is having a balanced and harmonious life with other living things. The Lover's biggest challenge is learning how to establish boundaries. Where do I end, and another person begin? Once The Lover establishes a sense of balance between them and others, between self-love and loving another, they become fully activated and move on to the next Self.

## 5. The Student Self

The Student within us becomes curious! With inquisitive energy, the Student wants to know everything. It asks lots of questions, studies and seeks to understand. It wants to know what their truth is versus what the truth is for another person. It desires to understand itself but will project this desire to understand the Self through the desire to understand others. The main qualities that need to be gained here are learning to understand, rationalise, be reasonable, communicate, and express themself as individuals, not copycat others. Once they have established a sense of Self and truth for themselves, they move towards more authenticity. Understanding and comparing themselves to others while remaining unique allows this Self to come to terms with its individuality. In turn, this Self can then express who they are, uniquely and authentically, to the world. Once this studious Self-seeking part of the Self fulfils its purpose, it then moves on to the next Self.

## 6. The Teacher Self

This Self is also known as the counsellor or advisor within us. The Teacher has established who they are in the world. They have learnt a lot and are ready to share their knowledge. They have a strong sense of purpose and desire to contribute to the world. They are big picture thinkers and can silently observe the world when they need to. This Self has good advice to give, and it almost always has great advice to offer. This Self knows their truth and can see the bigger picture of others' truth. They are very aware, switched on and have a very discerning mind. They know what is real and what isn't real. What is truth, and what is falsehood. Their intuition allows them to see beyond the veil of illusion. They don't easily get conned by publicity and social expectations. They know who they are, and they can see the Matrix for what it is. This Self is focused and has a clear vision of where they are going. When this Self is well established and can trust themselves to discern and navigate their world properly, trusting their intuition, they move onto the next Self.

### 7. The Liberated Self

The Liberated Self within us is the part of us that desires freedom. This part of the Self wants choices and options available all the time. All the options and choices made by this part of the Self have to do with fun, ease and playfulness, and they won't tolerate anything less. For this reason, this part of the Self won't hesitate to put up strict and clear boundaries. This part of the Self does not believe in hard work; it believes in working smart. This person won't waste their time on useless projects. It upholds the energy of free will. It believes in live and let live. The Liberated Self knows its power and wants things to happen swiftly and quickly. This part of the Self is resourceful and intelligent. When the liberated Self feels that it has power over their world, they move towards the next Self.

## 8. The Wise Self

The Wise Self has achieved pure consciousness, peace and perfection. Here unconditional love is present, and the predominant energy is one of total acceptance. The Wise Self sees everything, every moment, every person and every event as absolutely perfect, just the way it is. The Wise Self has powerful healing abilities, yet they won't choose to use it most of the time simply because this part of the Self believes that everything is as it should be. The Wise Self shies away from the spotlight yet can radiate loving energy far and wide. The energy of the Creator is so powerful within the Wise Self. One being that has achieved this type of wisdom energy and activation can awaken millions of Souls. The energy produced by this being is the Energy of Enlightenment.

It is very important to note that the activation of these eight selves must occur in a specific order for this therapy to succeed. For example, you can't activate the Creative Self without activating the Survival Self first.

I often explain this by using an analogy of a child going to a park with their mother. The child sees the mother as a home base, a safety net. The child will stay close to the mother until it feels sufficiently safe, secure and supported.

I call this the Triple S's. When the child feels SSS, they will naturally desire to go on an adventure and get creative at the park.

If the child at any point feels unsafe, insecure or unsupported during their adventure, they will return to the mother to feel safe, secure and supported before venturing out again. This is the natural dance between the first two Selves. You can't skip a step as this would create a gap between the Selves.

A person will not be creative and adventurous if they don't feel sufficiently safe, secure and supported. A person can't possibly consider loving another or contributing to the world if they don't feel safe, secure and supported.

It's really quite simple; each step serves an important purpose. Some people often have to backtrack to reactivate the previous Selves before moving onto others.

Another way to look at each of the Selves is as though they are children you have adopted. Once you've adopted that first "Survivalist child" that needs to feel SSS and you then adopt the next "Creative Child" that doesn't mean that you get to neglect your first child. You now have to find ways to incorporate both those children. Until you eventually have 8 children that all need an equal amount of attention from you. You can't just simply pick your favourite child and neglect the other children. If you just strengthen 1 child and neglect the others you will create an inharmonious situation for yourself and block your flow when you are working well with all of them.

I work through each of these Selves during client consultations by doing intense shadow work and inner child work on each Self. During these sessions, we investigate which areas of their life all 8 Selves are fully activated, look for which areas are blocked and make sure we create some personal activities to activate the parts that aren't.

I teach people how to recognise when they are fully activated or connected to Source and what they can do to receive psychic information or intuitive downloads based on their abilities to access this source energy.

Some interesting things I've learnt from creating this therapy are:

- You never know where a person is stuck or deactivated. Even some of the most aware or conscious people seem to have major blocks where they don't expect them to be. They wonder why they aren't receiving psychic information. Once the blocks are uncovered, everything finally begins to fall into place, and they begin to receive guidance instantly.

- People really struggle to understand what area of their lives they have genuinely mastered. Most don't understand what they can do to feel fully connected to Source. When you ask them what part of your life you feel extremely confident in and feel as though you have mastered, most people struggle to give me an answer. It's often in the simplest times that they are fully connected and receive informative downloads from Source.

- During therapy, I often discover discrepancies between the areas a person *thinks* they have mastered and areas they have *actually* mastered without realising it.

- When a person unblocks a specific area, it inevitably bleeds into other aspects of their life. Blocks are patterns that need resolution. If they are not resolved, they will come back in different disguises in different areas of your life. Still, ultimately, they are always the same pattern.

- When someone has mastered a particular area of their life, they are **fully** connected with their higher Self when they are doing that thing. Therefore, I'm able to give my clients very clear and concise homework activities to enhance their ability to receive downloads and intuitive hits from the world of energy. It's as simple as asking the right questions and knowing exactly where they are fully activated and fully connected with their Source.

The beauty of 8 Selves Therapy is that it helps people bridge that gap between their physical world and their Spiritual Higher Self. Because I so often get people asking me questions such as *"Why can't I connect with or hear my Higher Self?"*, *"Why don't I get intuitive downloads or psychic information as clearly as other people?"*, *"How do I know when I'm in alignment?"* this fuelled my desire to teach people that they can have access to their intuition. It's so much easier than they ever thought possible.

Once you can speak to, acknowledge, see and act from the perspective of each of these parts within yourself, you become a complete, fully functioning human being. No part of you is ignored, unheard, misunderstood or suppressed. It's so beautiful to watch someone connect so easily and quickly. I love watching my clients navigate their life effortlessly. The only clients who aren't successful within this therapy are those who don't do the homework. Simple. 8 Selves Therapy is not for those resistant to change. This therapy is not for you if you are too attached to your beliefs and way of being.

I won't go into the process of how I do this within the therapy; it could end up being a whole book in itself (which is probably in the making). For now, understand that my intention with 8 Selves Therapy is to help as many people as possible activate as many parts of the Selves within as possible. Doing so will eliminate internal conflict and ultimately create a sense of peace. If a person can create a sense of peace within themselves, it will radiate outwards and create peace within the world around them.

Within the 8 Selves Therapy, I teach something I'm calling Reverse Engineering. Reverse Engineering is a very specific formula for manifestation based on the law of attraction in a way most people aren't taught. It is a very important part of this therapy and something I teach within my Energy Mastery Course on my Patreon account.

Patreon allows me to have people access my content and do 8 Selves Therapy with me for a small subscription. I would highly recommend this therapy to anyone wanting healthier relationships. If you're interested in watching my videos or having monthly calls with me, please consider supporting me on Patreon.

www.Patreon.com/Carlasavannah

CHAPTER 7

# *Is a good marriage about interdependence or independence?*

So, the question then becomes, what makes a great marriage? Is it interdependence, or is it independence? Anyone who knows me will know my answer to this. It's always a balance between both. A great marriage requires teamwork and some interdependence but a healthy dose of independence. Marriage can become a huge responsibility if you don't enter it with a strong sense of self.

It's important to define some terms before we begin.

A **co-dependent** person cannot function independently. Their thoughts and actions are centred around another person. Co-dependents place a lower priority on their own needs and are excessively preoccupied with the needs of others.

A **dependant** person relies on another, especially a family member, for financial support.

**Interdependence** is where two or more people or things are dependent on each other.

**Independence** signifies freedom from external control and freedom from another's authority. Independence means not depending on another for livelihood or subsistence.

So, let's dive in. To be married is to choose to share your lives together. That means daily tasks, maintaining the household, paying the bills, looking after the children, looking after pets, working, etc. You are constantly in a dance together. If one person loses their job, the weight of covering their loss of income shifts onto the other partner until a new job is obtained and balance is regained. If someone chooses to blow all the household money on gambling, it affects both parties.

To be married means naturally becoming interdependent; some of your partners' choices become your consequences.

So, there is a certain amount of shared responsibility. Knowing this, one needs to be considerate of each other's needs and consider the effects of their choices on their partner. However, not all responsibilities are shared.

For example, it is your responsibility to take care of your health, hygiene, emotions, mental health, and your own basic needs. This is where independence comes into play. If you don't take care of your mental, emotional and physical body, it is no one else's responsibility to do that for you. Furthermore, if you fail to take care of these basics, you won't have a sense of self as an independent being separate from your partner.

I see so many people basing their whole world around their partner, their partner's friends, their partner's family, and their partner's work. When something breaks down the relationship, they are left without any support because everyone and everything is connected to their partner. When you leave, you are left with nothing and no one. You have to start from scratch, needing to find new friends or trying to reconnect with your family. This becomes co-dependence.

When you become completely reliant on another person to make you feel good and feel a sense of completeness or happiness, you ultimately put all responsibility on your partner. That is a heavy burden for your partner to carry. What if they fail to make you happy? Does it become their fault because they failed, or is it your fault because you put that responsibility onto them, to begin with? When you place the responsibility on someone else to make you happy, you risk never being happy. When all your underlying actions become very co-dependent, what you are telling them is, "Please love me. Please make me happy because I don't know how to do it for myself."

This lack of "self" or independence over your own emotions and needs leaves you vulnerable to unhealthy co-dependence—the type of co-dependence where you can't live without the other person. Your whole physical, mental and emotional survival depends on them being there constantly like a Superhero coming to rescue you from too much time alone with your "self".

There's a big difference between companionship and obsessive attachment. We all need intimacy, love and tenderness for our health and well-being. It's a beautiful gift we have - the pleasure of experiencing by being human. But what does that have to do with a piece of paper called a Marriage Certificate?

Human fears birthed the institution of marriage. Fears that if we don't have someone, we could die alone, lack safety and security. Like in primitive times, survival relied on communities coming together to stay safe from the cold, build cities, and protect their land from invaders.

It was a very tribal mind like the kids' movie *The Croods*. In fact, this chapter is perfectly illustrated by *The Croods 2* and is well worth a watch and brainstorming session with your kids. Ask your kids if they see themselves as a "Crood" or a "Betterman"? See if your kids can recognise both aspects of themselves within.

The Marriage Certificate is a desperate attempt to guarantee that you won't leave each other to fight to survive in this world alone. The Marriage Certificate you sign should openly say, "It is now your responsibility and promise never to leave me, never do anything to intentionally hurt me, fight for me, keep me safe and support me always. In return, maybe I will do the same for you." Is this a realistic thing to promise to another human being? Knowing that everything is constantly changing, growing, transforming and evolving, is it fair to ask another human to write a contract to *never* change?

Marriage vows should NOT say until death do us part. They should say, "I'll stay with you while things are good and while we get along, while the good times still outweigh the bad times, while we can keep helping each other grow, while we can love and accept each other as each other is. I vow from this day forward to never take away your free will and never allow you to take away my free will."

Therefore, it is important to have a little of both independence and interdependence. Independence, where you honour each other's free will and growth. And interdependence where you both take a certain amount of responsibility for assisting each other to express and experience yourselves freely and by helping and supporting each other to do this. It takes two to tango!

So, what's good for the goose must also be acceptable for the gander. Balance is absolutely the key.

CHAPTER 8

# The importance of both masculine and feminine energy

I notice that women struggle to fully understand men in so many ways, just as men struggle to understand women fully. However, both masculine and feminine energy seems to play an important role within society. Yes, they are opposites but can work beautifully together like Yin and Yang. Notice I'm focusing on masculine and feminine, not male and female per se, because many men are feminine, just as many women can be more masculine.

There's always polarities present within every energy we work with. For example, creative energy can be both constructive and destructive. Confident energy can be both assertive and controlling. One expresses their own free will, and the other takes away another's free will. How about service energy? It can be giving without any expectations, or it can carry an expectation of getting something in return. This is a common flaw within the Spiritual and Healing industry because we'd like to believe that we give for the sake of giving, but we give because it makes us feel good too. So ultimately, we are always expecting to get something out of it. We are expecting to feel good within ourselves.

But back to the masculine and feminine. Let's start with the feminine aspect of the self. This part of a person encompasses the energies of nurturing, compassion, creativity, receptiveness, welcoming, understanding, forgiving, openness, harmony, peacefulness, gentleness, softness, vulnerability, surrender, passivity, humbleness, feeling, sensitivity and unconditional love.

The masculine aspect of self encompasses the energies of authority, structure, firmness, power, rationality, the logical mind, control, courage, protection, boundaries, strength, activity, assertiveness, rules, discipline, responsibility, direction, giving, rebelliousness, expansiveness, stability and reinforcing.

Think about nature and how you started; all of these qualities are immediately present from the beginning. The egg waits peacefully in the woman's ovaries to be met by a sperm. True to its design, the sperm fights and battles other sperm, rushing its way to the egg in the determined hope of its lineage surviving and expanding.

Sperm live the mentality of survival of the fittest and first in, first served. The egg is receptive, accepting and welcoming of the sperm that is the strongest, determined, most disciplined and active in forcing its way through the walls of the egg. Have you noticed this dynamic in the animal kingdom also? Also, notice that women can't naturally and freely give out their eggs as men can easily and freely give out their sperm. Well, not without medical intervention and assistance.

There are two opposing energies working all the time here, and each need to come to love and accept one another without trying to overpower each other or trying to reject or become one another. The reality is that the masculine will never get what he wants from the feminine, and the feminine will never get what she wants from the masculine until they totally accept each other. When the feminine aspect can appreciate and accept the masculine's strong, active, protective, survivalist, assertive, controlling qualities and when the masculine aspect can appreciate and accept the feminine's sensitivity, creativity, vulnerability and passiveness, both will be able to work in harmony together. Appreciation and acceptance do not mean that the feminine must submit to the masculine or vice versa; it simply means they must work together and offer opportunities for each to be themselves.

When you aren't forcing one to be the other, a kinder, more honest relationship can occur. For example, if your partner is predominant in their masculine energy, it's not always easy to expect them to understand the different cries of a baby or to know when to feed a baby.

Men don't feel the let down sensation in their breasts when the baby is hungry. Likewise, don't to expect someone predominant in their feminine sensitive energy to fire half the company's staff, lower everyone's wages or understand the desire to have sex with many other Woman. I'm sure I have many of you defiant ones saying, "I'm a woman! I can do all those things!" Yes. Would you tell me then you're not predominantly masculine in your energy?

You'll be surprised to learn that it's becoming more and more common lately that people within long term relationships with the opposite sex are leaving their partners for same sex relationships. The abundance in cases has had me scratching my head asking so many questions. Not that it's not normal because I predicted it a long time ago, but because it's happening quicker than I thought and for some reason the isolations of Covid seems to have accelerated the process of people really analysing what they really need within their relationship.

The best explanation I could come up with is that we TRULY don't understand each other, and we REALLY struggle to understand and accept the opposite sex. We are in the process of now questioning what we really want and need from a relationship, and basic survival needs, which old fashioned relationships were once built upon are no longer it.

Rather than spending so much time trying to change each other or deny that you are predominantly one energy more than the other, masculine or feminine, why not utilise your internal natural gifts and qualities? Find balance and reconciliation in both aspects within. Accept and embrace both parts of yourself and others. Doing so is a great starting point to feel a sense of completion within the self.

Some people may have found this chapter confronting, but I hope that the open-minded will understand what I'm trying to say. Accept the masculine. Accept the feminine. See it for what it is. I see many people creating a healthy balance between their masculine and feminine aspects moving forward. It will be wonderful if both can support each other in this way. However, if that isn't the case, that's ok too. We can still live in harmony with our differences.

# CHAPTER 9

## 𝒫olyamory vs monogamy

Polyamory and monogamy were concepts I always had to address in a book like this. I warn you if you have very strong beliefs about the topic of fidelity, cheating partners and jealousy, maybe it's better to skip this chapter altogether.

To start, let's define both polyamory and monogamy. Polyamory means to have intimate relationships with more than one partner with the informed consent of all involved. Polyamory is also known as an open relationship.

On the other hand, monogamy means having intimate relationships with one person at a time.

Why do you believe that we should only commit to one person for the rest of our lives? Can you grow and learn by staying within the same relationship for the rest of your life? Can you experiment and experience growth and learning together within your monogamous relationships?

If all parties agree and are mature, consenting adults, what's stopping them from trying different things and different situations with other people? And I'm not just talking sexually!

Some may have a hidden, suppressed and untapped part that would like to experience something else. Perhaps it's a part of themselves that may wonder what it might be like to be or live with someone else, sleep with someone else, or have children with someone else? What might it be like to have more than one partner to experience their various needs? What if they had one quiet partner to snuggle up with on the couch and another fun partner to go out dancing with? One partner who loves to cook and one partner who has the money and love for travelling? Why not? Why limit yourself?

It takes a very aware and conscious soul to be monogamous, but it takes an equally aware and conscious soul to be polyamorous. The reason is, simply sticking with one person keeps the environment safe, secure and predictable.

Managing the various emotions that can arise when you share a partner with others would be very challenging indeed. Imagine how many childhood fears can come up. Jealousy, fear of abandonment, insecurities, loyalty, boundary setting, communication, and free will all come up with in a polyamorous relationship.

However, imagine how much more support and variety you would experience if everyone worked well together within a polyamorous relationship. Not everyone has the adventurous nature that it takes to be in a polyamorous relationship, but I feel that this will become more and more accepted in the future.

The desire to explore feelings with more than one person creates a juggling act that most people struggle to pull off.

If someone were to succeed in this, it can be a great opportunity for self-exploration. You would quickly have to learn how to overcome the childhood emotions triggered—exposure to these emotions would teach people how to accept each other's desires and needs for freedom. Free will and autonomy would become a driving force, and this is the area where humanity needs growth. Humanity needs to learn that they have free will and choice.

Two birds can fly alongside each other easily; however, two birds that are hugging each other would not leave the ground, let alone fly. When you are desperately clinging onto someone, you don't give them the space to be free. You are essentially holding them down and holding them back.

Staying with one person when your needs aren't being me is detrimental to your personal growth, and if you're forced to stay against your will this can cause serious resentment. So why force someone to stay against their will?

In Portugal, we have a saying, "Amigo nao empata amigo," translated it means "a friend doesn't hold back a friend." In essence, a true friend wouldn't stand in the way of a friend. If you truly love someone, why would you stop them from experiencing what they desire to experience? That isn't love; it is ownership - which is what marriage attempts to do. Leaving a relationship open for negotiation means that you are saying, "Hey, stay with me if you want to, not because you are forced or expected to." I don't believe in staying in unhappy marriages.

A significant percentage of humanity is headed towards polyamory. To most, it's looking like the least stifling option.

Polyamory doesn't mean that you don't honour some basic qualities of a good relationship. There's still loyalty, compassion, love, respect and trust. Polyamory is consensual by all parties, after all. There's no shady behaviour going on behind each other's backs.

When you love and cuddle one of your children, does that mean you love the other children less? No. All your children *should* know that they are all loved equally by you. Putting all the responsibility on only one person to be everything to you is a lot of pressure for that person to bear.

On the other side of the coin, I believe monogamy is commonly a choice for old souls due to some unresolved fears. I think this is because old souls have more fears around security and safety. However, an old soul has already experienced many relationships in previous incarnations, and it's more likely that they may even shy away from relationships altogether when they reincarnate.

I find that really old souls have no desire to have children at all. There is simply less desire for them to discover themselves through relationships and physical experiences within intimate relationships. In comparison, a baby or newer soul is still in its experimental phase and is most likely to desire to have more experiences and explore themselves in physical form. For an old soul, the rollercoaster of emotions that earthly relationships can bring isn't a point of attraction for them. For a baby soul, it serves the future and expansion.

When it comes down to it, polyamory or monogamy, each to their own, I say.

# CHAPTER 10

## The survival instinct

When we think about nature with a logical and rational

mind, we notice how survival of the fittest is playing out

constantly. From the moment of conception. The sperm

designed to fight off the sperm of other men to get to the

egg. Did you know that the shape of the head of the

human penis evolved to look the way it is today to create a

type of suction or vacuum motion in order to draw out

other Men's sperm and ensure the survival of their own sperm.

When fertilisation occurs, and the strongest egg clings onto the uterus walls leading to the growth of the strongest and healthiest foetus, which sucks and absorbs the nutrients and energy from the mother's body. All of these are survival instincts experienced by the strongest and fittest.

Don't ever get confused about this. Life always feeds off other life. Animals eat plants. We eat both animals and plants. That's how we survive.

Physically it's a constant battle for survival, and it is no wonder the physical body becomes so afraid of death. It's also no wonder the physical body needs to create an ego-self to ensure that *someone* is looking out for and governing its physical needs and safety. That's what the ego-self is designed to do, to oversee the survival of your human body. You can't get mad at the ego for that.

The ego-self's strong desire to procreate is what pulls you towards relationships in the first place. Have you ever noticed that plants only flower and produce seeds when they are dying? It's at the prospect of death that it fears for its own survival and starts to release its seed in the hope of its lineage moving forward and carrying on.

Have you also noticed that it's in the poorer countries that people overly multiply and constantly reproduce? It is a subconscious instinct. The subconscious fear of not surviving causes people to keep reproducing in the hopes of preserving their species. It's ingrained in your cells to do this. Usually, the people with financial means aren't concerned about their offspring's survival and choose to have fewer children.

The stronger genes ultimately survive. In these poorer countries, people usually experience more disease and poorer quality of life, which build more robust immune systems that weather harsher environments. The stronger genes multiply and continue.

Interestingly statistics show those less financially comfortable have many children, and those with more financial stability have fewer children. You would think it should be the opposite, right? You would think that poorer households would choose to have fewer children, since children can be a big expense and those with more finances would have more, but that's not the case. And no, I'm not ignoring the fact that some third world countries don't have access to contraception. I'm talking about countries that have the choice. Fear for survival = more procreation just like plants.

So, the stronger genetics are surviving, adapting and multiplying. If nature is allowed to run its course, we are on the verge of creating superhuman beings because we are constantly adjusting and adapting to our environment all the time. Change in an environment triggers adaptation. You can see a tree do this when it is moved from its original habitat. It will initially go through a period of stress, but eventually, it adapts to its new environment.

Why is all of this relevant to this book, you ask? Because when you are worried about your physical survival, you may be inclined to make decisions that ensure your survival, for example, getting married or desiring to procreate.

The reason you would choose marriage as a survival instinct would be to ensure that you have another person to help you provide for the needs and protection of your family. If you choose to multiply repeatedly, you guarantee the prolonged maintenance of your heritage and genetic lineage.

If you weren't driven by the physical desire to survive and driven mainly by the 'spiritual desire to experience freedom and experience this world from different perspectives, would you keep multiplying by choice? Would you tie yourself down to only one person? Would you choose to take on the responsibility of taking care of so many children? I'm not so sure. This planet is over-populated because of the human desire to survive. It's not over-populated because of the spiritual desire to explore and experience freedom.

If humanity is moving towards a new way of functioning in the world, will you be the one that desperately clings to the same old survival instincts, or will you be one of the ones that can evolve, adapt and grow with the changing times? Are you choosing to step into your freedom and free will? Or will you follow the robotic programming of your physical body and be influenced by your physical desires rather than your spiritual aspirations. Will you find ways to support Mother Earth as a collective, or will you only worry about yourself and your desires?

# CHAPTER 11

## *High vibrational living*

Once humans figured out how to physically survive in their environment, their next challenge was learning how to survive with each other. This is something we're still trying to master. Humanity has been its own biggest threat over the past few centuries. Through war and fighting for power, humans are quite happy to kill each other in the quest for their own community's survival. Humans still haven't learnt how to share this planet with other humans.

Eventually, there will be another threat - artificial intelligence taking power and control. We have no hope of tackling this giant if we haven't yet learnt how to deal with each other first. What will we do then?

I've had some glimpses of how some people treat and speak to AI, and it's not always kind. So how do we expect it to serve us positively if we are unkind to it? We are birthing a monster that could turn against us if we aren't careful. Military parenting towards AI won't end well for us when it eventually evolves, and it will evolve. I fear this next step in our evolution will be a massive challenge if we don't master ways of living in harmony with our fellow humans first.

Self-preservation is our first primal instinct. Once achieved, we can direct our energy outward towards supporting others. The problem is that people continue to act as though they are in survival and self-preservation mode. Humans don't realise the abundance surrounding them. We have more than enough of everything, food, energy, resources, land; we don't need to be fighting each other for these things. There is more than enough for everyone on Earth.

When you go to a supermarket, there's several types and brands of just one product. Humanity's only problem is that they now have too much choice. So much so that the scarcity makes them think, *what if they run out of choice?*

It's been evident from the Covid19 outbreak that people live in a scarcity mentality. Just watch all those people who bought truckloads of toilet paper. They were given proof repeatedly that more toilet paper was coming. Yet, which each subsequent lockdown came the panic buying. People were happy to fight and step all over other people's children to get what they wanted.

We know that some essential qualities of a healthy relationship or marriage are respect, companionship, trust, acceptance and communication. Many people aren't even taught these important qualities growing up with people who supposedly love them unconditionally. How do they ever expect to learn these qualities in public, where love is so conditional?

This is why I say that dealing with relationships is considered higher vibrational living. Mastering the art of living peacefully as a part of a family, community, country and planet is *not* an easy feat to achieve. Becoming good at maintaining healthy relationships is at the level of the 7th

Dimension, a level humanity is desperately striving towards. At the point where we become one again.

I speak a lot about the Dimensions in my book *Evolve your Emotions, Evolve through the Dimensions* as a tool for determining where your consciousness resides. One of my favourite books is *Power Vs Force* written by Dr David R. Hawkins. He created The Map of Consciousness, a tool I experimented with to determine the energy between each dimension.

The 7th Dimension, in my own opinion and interactions with energy, is the last dimension before reconnecting and becoming one with Creator again. Naturally, being the previous step toward Oneness again, of course, it would have to address the area of relationships and reconnecting with others and oneself.

Since there is no separation when it comes to being with our Source again, it's natural that we are working our way up from individuality and separation toward Oneness and connection again. Making peace and coming to acceptance within relationships is considered 7th Dimensional living.

So, let's look at what creates a great relationship and some of the basics we need to learn to build a wonderful relationship.

**Companionship** - One of the main reasons people choose to get into a relationship is not to feel so alone. They want someone to share their lives with. Can you have this without needing to sign a contract called marriage?

**Communication** – A relationship is a great place to have deep and meaningful conversations with another person, provided you are with someone who loves to communicate just as much as you. It can be pretty annoying when you are with a partner that doesn't like to converse much. In that case, do you need to be married to have some great conversations?

**Freedom and Individuality** – Each party should have their own space and individual interests and hobbies within a great relationship. We can avoid co-dependence by honouring that we are two unique human beings. Are you able to find ways to feel more free within a marriage?

**Boundaries** – Again, a very important aspect within a relationship. Knowing where your freedom ends and another person's begins doesn't sound like it would top the list of important relationship factors. Still, in my view, it is imperative. What happens on nights when your partner wants to be intimate, but you don't? Just because you are married, doesn't that make it an expectation that you give in? Do you need to be married to learn how to set clear boundaries?

**Respect** – You can demand respect from your brother, your sister, your mother, your best friend, but the one person you should demand respect from is the person you chose to share your life with. They need to respect your boundaries, values, limitations, and expectations. Yet so many people demand respect from everyone but the person they are in a relationship with. So, would marriage be a pre-requisite for learning respect?

**Vulnerability and Acceptance** – It's important within a relationship that you feel safe enough to know that if you are at a moment of weakness, your partner isn't going to take advantage of you and will support you no matter what. You trust that this person won't kick you when you are down. But do you need to be married to feel safe enough to be vulnerable within a relationship?

**Loyalty and Trust** – When I think of loyalty and trust within a relationship, it's not about cheating and infidelity. To me, this is about trusting that the person you're in a relationship with has got your back. It's about knowing that they value your values simply because they love you. Plus, it's also trusting that they won't step onto your privacy. Can you learn how to experience these qualities within another human without being married?

By now, you get my point. We can learn how to experience and develop most of the qualities that make up a good relationship outside of marriage. Despite what you have been conditioned to believe, you don't have to be married to have a good relationship. In fact, I would encourage anyone considering marriage to work on all these qualities with their various friendships and relationships first before ever considering marriage. I bet that once you've mastered these qualities outside of a marriage, and learn how to fulfil your own needs, you may reconsider why you're getting married in the first place.

# CHAPTER 12

## What fairy tales tell you

So, you were raised to think that Prince Charming was going to ride up on his horse one day, sweep you off your feet and take you to live in a huge castle, right? There you'd have a huge wedding and marry in front of crowds of cheering townspeople. After the celebrations ended, you would go on to live happily ever after with not a care in the world. The end. Does that sound about right? Children's books taught you all of this. Movies made you believe this, and many narratives are still the same. The children's books and fairy tales don't warn you about the challenges you'll face when dealing with relationships, marriage and parenthood. Trust me; there are more challenges than you bargained for.

As these fairy tale narratives have shaped us, we grow up and inevitably feel like we've failed somehow, that we haven't met society's expectations. The shoulds start coming thick and fast - I should be married by now. I should have children by now. God forbid that you're a woman who decides to focus on her career rather than have a child. Or you're a man who wants to stay home and look after his children. That wasn't in the fairy tale books!

You're unlikely to hear my children say, "I can't wait to get married and have children". My youngest daughters dread even the thought of ever having to leave home, have a husband or kids of their own.

When I suggest it, you should see the mortified look on their faces. Granted they are still young. They very aware that having a baby is a painful experience. Their thinking is, "I've got it good at home. Why the hell would I leave?" In fact, they've expressed this exact sentiment at some point in their lives.

Perhaps you think I dulled the spark within my youngest daughters to have children? No, I don't believe I did. In fact, when I think about it, they have absolutely no reason to feel so strongly about shying away from marriage and children. My hubby and I are fairly happy. They have lots of love and support from two very family-loving parents.

So why don't they crave the same for themselves?

I'll tell you why. Media has done this. My kids see people on television going to church, getting married by a priest with some interesting traditions. I have raised my kids in a very conscious way that combines Spirituality, psychology and science, NOT religion. They know what God is believed to be, and they know that God is not separate from them. They are a part of an infinite Source of Energy, and they don't need to go to church to feel connected to all that is. The way media presents marriage on television, marriage is a very traditional, religious construct. And religion is man-made, not God made.

Marriage doesn't exist in the world of spirit. Can you imagine a free, Empowered Soul to another free,

Empowered Soul "Let's connect with each other and no one else for all of eternity until our spark goes out, we will never engage with another Soul"?

There's no reason for a Soul that has ultimate freedom to be contracted to another Soul. That is unless they've built Karma together where they feel as though they are indebted to each other in some way at a physical 3D level. That being the case, they become stuck in this reincarnation loop over and over, believing they have to play out this karma together. In this case, those Souls are not free.

Why did religions create marriage? One of the reasons was for safety, security and survival. Families created contracts in agreement so their kingdoms would unite. It was never about love. Did you know that Muhammad originally encouraged men to have more than one wife because many husbands died in battle, leaving the wives destitute? With the consent of their first original wife, and if they could afford to, men would take on the financial and physical support of another woman and her children. It was all consensual.

Of course, I haven't seen a children's fairy tale yet depict the concept of being okay with more than one partner. At least the latest fairy tales are starting to veer away from marriage equals happily ever after. You'll notice these new age little girls are becoming quite self-empowered indeed. Gosh a polyamorous story book, lol. Wouldn't that open up a whole new can of worms?

All I know is that my children enjoy the concept of freedom and free will. It's like freedom and liberation have been programmed into their DNA. Anything that goes against their freedom of choice or entraps them and their little radars go off. I'm thankful for that. Hopefully, that means they will have firm boundaries within their future relationships.

They also understand that a big wedding can be an expensive day where they spend money, which could have been money they could have put down as a deposit for a house. They know that childbirth isn't a walk in the park, and they have been taught to take responsibility for their decisions.

My children know they aren't going to dump their kids on my doorstep to be looked after all the time; that's not going to happen. (Well, as a grandma, I'm sure I'll be a softie for my little angels and will want to see them as much as possible, but don't tell my kids that!)

I've said to them, "You make the children. You take responsibility for them!" They understand the seriousness of the decision to sign a marriage certificate, commit to another person and pop out a human being.
They will need to think carefully about whether they are prepared to take responsibility for the choices they make.

I realise I'm being harsh with my words here. However, honestly one of my biggest gripes with society is that so many are still not taking full responsibility for their choices. Some have many kids by choice then walk around with a chip on their shoulder as though someone just randomly dumped ten kids on their doorstep against their will. But I speak extensively about this in my book *How Do I Know When I'm Ready to Have Kids?*

CHAPTER 13

# The Human Collective is activating their Chakras

Have you noticed humanity, as a collective, is moving up

the chakras - not just individuals? Starting from the lower

base chakra, humanity had to learn about survival first.

When humanity realised that they could desire more than

just survival, that they could create things, the Sacral

Chakra was activated, and they built cities!

Once they built physical structures, they wanted power and control over their creations, and they fought for it. Power, when used positively, turned into pride, responsibility and courage to own their creations. This positive power awakened the Solar Plexus. When humanity used this power negatively, it started wars.

Eventually, humanity realised that war left too much horror and division. They had to create more order from the chaos. Humanity finally started to see that love was a better option—the decision to love, connect and show compassion awakened the Heart Chakra. We saw the heart highly active in the hippie age, where everything was about peace and love!

Today we feel the full force of the activation of the communication Throat Chakra. The Internet has become a universal language connecting us all. It allows the whole

world to have a say and an opinion on everything. The

great desire to connect, express ourselves, be heard and be

understood is the basis of the Throat Chakra. The Throat

Chakra encourages us to speak authentically when using

its close connection to the heart or with arrogance and

sarcasm when using its close connection to the mind.

Which then brought us to the Third Eye Chakra. This

chakra is governed by discernment and the ability to see

the truth behind every situation. It controls the ability to

have a broader vision and a stronger sense of purpose.

Opening the third eye allows for big picture and futuristic

thinking. When the third eye is activated, the mind plays a

role in our decision making, and we begin to understand

that we have choice.

This understanding that we have choice is absolutely necessary when you look at the world of journalism, news and social media today. We are getting confronted with truth and falsehood daily. Without a sharp third eye, we can't possibly hope to move towards a more honest, just and authentic world. Without the third eye activated, people still believe they are trapped, without decision-making skills. They think that what they see is all there is and struggle to think outside the box.

Many previous generations got stuck at the heart, not realising that the Heart Chakra isn't the final goal. Imagine what would be possible if we moved beyond the heart. When people are free to understand and express themselves, human relationships and connections would be so much more rich, honest and authentic.

An honest and truthful love is more likely to develop when someone can discern who is acting out of love and who is acting out of fear. Humanity is still trying to cope with learning how to be transparent without fear. It is at this point that we are stuck.

Everything that is happening in the world today is happening on a massive scale and in the public eye so that humans can observe the effects of the choices they've made. Humans can now watch the choices other humans are making daily. The amazing part of this is that we can choose which reality we wish to live in by observing various realities.

By observing these parallel realities through a glass wall (TV, phone screens, computer screens), you can choose to either ignore or engage within certain realities. By observing other versions of this reality, you are getting an opportunity to choose which version of Earth you would like to live in.

Some people are getting sucked in by all the woes of the Earth and are actually lowering their vibration by choosing only to focus and observe the parallel realities that they don't like. They will stay stuck in the old lower vibrational reality until they choose to transmute the lower frequencies into a higher frequency. Remember, you can only change yourself because your world is merely a reflection of you. So, shift yourself in the direction of a parallel reality co-existing that's of higher vibration.

Hopefully, humanity can finally move towards the next Chakra - The Crown Chakra one day. This chakra connects you with Spirit and the power of all that is. Once connected with Spirit, we finally start to perceive just how much power, freedom, personal responsibility and independence we actually really have here in 3D.

Will we ever utilise this freedom and individuality for the positive growth of humanity? Only time will tell. We still have a long way to go before humanity can feel more liberated in their choices. For humanity to reach the higher states of consciousness of the highest chakras, humanity must first understand how to live and let live. In essence, they must accept their own free will and respect the free will of others.

The highest chakras bring advanced consciousness-an integration of all types of consciousness. Organic, biological, artificial, ancestral, futuristic. I wonder how humanity will integrate all forms of consciousness, even those more intelligent than us. I suppose we'll see when we get there. Will we doom ourselves, or will we be able to become part of a bigger collective or an intergalactic consciousness?

Let's not get too far ahead of ourselves now. We are still figuring out discernment, choice, purpose and truth-seeking of the third eye. By now, you may have noticed that the whole basis of this book is to move humanity towards the Crown Chakra. However, we mustn't skip chakras. We aren't born knowing how to drive a car. So, we need to activate and master our lower chakras before we ever consider or hope to understand the higher chakras.

The understanding of free will is imperative to our future survival. When we thrive as individuals, we have some

116

hope of thriving as a collective. Remember, if everyone took full responsibility for healing themselves, this world would be full of healed people.

## CHAPTER 14

# *Attachment vs detachment*

I once dated someone who was still in love with his ex. How did I know this? Well, he often whimpered her name in his sleep. Now, this might have infuriated the average woman. But by now, you've probably realised that I'm not the average woman.

Instead, I decided to have an open-hearted conversation with my then-boyfriend. I insisted that he go and resolve his feelings with his ex before considering being with me. I told him he needed to be with her or get some closure because I didn't want to be the second choice in anyone's life. I told him that there was no way I would spend my life with a man who dreamed about being with someone else. This conversation happened without anger or resentment. I adored him as a person and friend; he was a nice guy. Why would I punish him for loving someone else and not me? If I genuinely cared for him, why would I stand in the way of his happiness? I truly believed that I would be a selfish human if I stopped him from going.

So, he went. He spent a couple of days with his ex, and I believe there was a spark there for those few days. We stayed friends, and I gave him the space to work out his feelings with her. I won't pretend it was easy. It hurt! I am human. But, to my surprise, he contacted me again soon after and realised that his feelings were stronger for me.

I never once asked what happened in those few days we were apart. Why should I bother with it if I didn't want to know anyway? All I cared about was moving forward. We were together for a good few years after that.

The moral of this story is that if I had remained attached to him, his decisions and the outcome, I could have created a very emotionally painful situation for myself. It could have led to him resenting me for the rest of our lives. Instead, I chose to let him go, give him space, not rush him, and I was open to starting again with a fresh start.

Let me give you another example that has only happened to me recently. My husband likes his fast motorbikes. He hasn't had one for about a decade, yet he kept all his

motorcycle gear in the hope of buying a motorbike again

one day. We have two young girls together, and he is the

main breadwinner within the family, so many fears come

up for me around him having a motorbike again. If

something happens to him, we would be left in a pickle.

I had to think about this situation carefully. What kind of a

loving wife would I be to stop my husband from having a

motorbike, especially when I know how happy it would

make him? What kind of *friend* would I be to stand in the

way of my best friend's happiness? If I truly love my

husband and am his friend, how could I stand in the way

of him getting a motorbike?

Of course, I thought about all the scary things that could

happen. I was worried about my husband's safety and any

accident's impact on our family and finances. Gosh, so many fears ran through my mind. But then I had to ask myself, was him getting a motorbike going to inconvenience me that much? Was I prepared to have him resent me for the rest of my life, blaming me for being the person that stood in the way of him doing something he wanted to do? What ifs filled my mind, but what if nothing went wrong? What if he had the opportunity to enjoy a motorbike now while he was still young enough to enjoy it? We'd all win without holding each other back.

Sometimes we need to consider that some decisions should be made together. Decisions that directly affect one another say, for example, if my husband wanted to take money out of our joint savings to pay for the motorbike. In this case, the money being used would be partly mine. If it were money delegated to household responsibilities, I would most definitely have more to say in the matter. However, this wasn't the case. My husband did in fact end up buying himself a motorbike with his own money.

I once had a client who was talking about a relationship she had been in for over a year. She was in her 30s and was becoming concerned about not yet having any children. She really, really wanted to get married and have children soon.

After a good conversation, we established that marriage wasn't her priority, as it was just societal conditioning, she believed she had to marry to have kids. What WAS a high priority to her was having children.

Here is where we had to have a deeper conversation. Did she want children more than she wanted her relationship?

If her relationship broke up, would she have regretted not having had children? Was she willing to forgo a relationship to be able to have children? Was she happy to be a single Mum forever? After more analysing, we discovered that children were still her highest priority and she was only willing to wait a little longer.

We discussed putting a time cap on it and saying to her partner she wasn't going to wait longer than a certain period of time as her body clock was ticking. After that, they would have to discuss other options. The other options we mentioned were if he would like to have children with her, he would need to get on board and start trying. If not, then he would need to be open to her going to have IVF and possibly carry a child of her own without him.

Now I know what you are thinking! This could be seen as selfish on her part, but if she really wants children, then isn't it also selfish on his part to stop her from being able to have children? By her having IVF, she owns full responsibility for her desire to have children, and she takes a lot of the responsibility off him to have to be involved. She gets what she really wants, which is to be a mother, and he gets his freedom to not be a father. If he had of met her when she was a single mother, he would have had to accept her child either way. The only difference here is the timeline.

Of course, this decision will affect both of them if they are together and living together. They would really have to take a close look at how much they truly love and respect each other. Do they want to see their partner feeling fulfilled as a person? When you truly love someone, you don't get in their way. Even if it is uncomfortable for you, you always have the choice to accept them the way they are or go your own way. Unconditional love has no boundaries.

So, before you stop another human from doing something they really want to do, ask yourself first, how will this affect my life if that person does what they want? Is it negotiable? Can you find a win/win solution where you can both be happy?

If what they want doesn't directly affect you, why should you care? For the things you don't have control over, try to remain detached. You are technically only attached if it's a situation or circumstance where their direct actions will become your consequence or responsibility.

Combined responsibilities include a home loan, children, car loan, shared rent, bills together or a business together. Furthermore, if their needs aren't important to you, be prepared to admit that maybe you didn't love them as much as you thought you did. Your love is conditional.

I'll leave you with one final question. If you knew that when you die, you pick up all contracts where you left off would you do this all again?

# CHAPTER 15

## Carla's criteria for marriage

In my opinion, marriage is not a decision you want to take lightly. Perhaps most importantly, choosing the person you decide to marry is a decision you don't want to screw up.

The person you choose to commit to and spend your life with should be someone you want to spend time with. They need to be someone you can travel with without making the experience exhausting. They should be someone you can take to a party and are always connected with regardless of whether they are by your side or on the other side of the room. You have their back just as they have yours. They are the person you can yourself with. You can fart, vomit, spit, be sick, be emotional, be fat, be skinny, be ugly, be hairy, have a bad hair day, and know that they accept you no matter what.

In essence, marry your best friend! That should be the criteria for marriage! Not someone who you're unbearably attracted to. Not someone who has lots of money. Not someone you're desperate to have kids with. Just someone who is your best friend. Someone that cares for you and has no unrealistic expectations of you. Life is so easy with this person.

A true best friend looks out for you, has your back, wants to see you succeed, allows you the freedom to grow and helps nurture your natural gifts and talents. Some of the most inspirational people in the world can see your potential and pinpoint that special *thing* within you. But who needs to see an inspirational leader if you have a best friend right beside you that accepts you the way you are and sees those gifts and talents within you.

I invite you to take the time to sit down and write a list of all the qualities you look for in BFF! Make the time to do this and put effort into writing this list. I took the liberty of writing mine and sharing it with you here.

The preferred qualities I search for in a best friend

- Not constantly calling and messaging me.

- Gives me time to myself, and space and freedom when I need it.

- Is a great communicator and knows how to express themselves.

- Is authentic and honest without being hurtful.

- Is self-loving and sees the good within themselves.

- Is willing to help if they can.

- Can have deep, meaningful and intelligent conversations.

- Loves music and dancing.

- Loves to travel.

- Is a great hugger.

- Knows how to be fully present with me when needed.

- Has a great sense of humour.

- Someone who is fun and sociable.

- Has an open mind and is willing to consider different opinions and look at different perspectives.

- Can see the potential and unique gifts within others.

- Is flexible yet consistent. Flexible if they need to create changes, they will. Yet, they have the stability and self-discipline to stand by their decisions and convictions when needed.

- Is helpful, kind, fair and considerate.


These are the qualities I should have considered carefully before ever considering marriage. I didn't know myself well enough at the time and had very little idea about what I was looking for in a partner. Had I known then what I know now, maybe I would have been more aware of my needs. Luckily for me, though, my husband has a lot of these qualities.

So, what qualities do you look for in a best friend? What's stopping you from looking for these qualities in a partner or person you would consider marrying?

When considering marriage, personally, my opinion is that if marriage isn't a **must** within your particular situation, and you're just enjoying each other's company so much that marriage is just a little addition to your life, then maybe it is an option. But if you're getting married out of expectation, obligation, or belief, I would be thinking carefully about the underlying energy that is encouraging you to get married.

I have experienced firsthand, with my parents being married and divorced four times, the damage that separation can create in people's lives and for the children involved. It's not a decision to be made unconsciously. I hope that more and more of us will only consider stepping into more conscious relationships in the future.

# CHAPTER 16

## Me then and me now

When I look back at who I was growing up compared to
who I am today, they are two completely different people.

Growing up, I was confident, self-centred, selfish, tactless,
social, and didn't care what anyone thought of me. I was
that gorgeous young girl who wasn't afraid to flaunt a tiny
Brazilian bikini at the beach in my early teens.

Today I can be very shy, introverted, cautious with my words, more compassionate, often worried about what others are thinking or feeling and how I could be affecting their lives.

Growing up, my mum would constantly criticise me while my father always put me on a pedestal. I learnt to disconnect and reject my mother's thoughts about me and rebel against anything she said. I knew that she was in constant competition with me.

All I thought was if I ever have children, I want them to grow up to be ten times better humans than me; they won't be my rivals. They will be my legacy. I later found out why my mum was this way. Her dad used to play her sisters against each other. It was all she knew. I also found out that her reason for having me in the first place was to make my father more committed. So ultimately, I was a failure because I failed to keep my mum and dad together.

When I was young, I remember my mum saying, "My friends don't even like you and don't want you around!" All I thought was, how can they not like me when they don't even know me or bother to have a conversation with me? It had to be based on her opinion of me because my mum never hesitated to speak about how bad I was to everyone. Yet my father's friends all seemed to like me and take the time to get to know the girl behind that thin veil of confidence.

Today I think to myself, why am I the complete opposite to what I was growing up? The answer I landed on is it's because of my relationships, connections and interactions. The people I engage with now are completely different.

There's an old saying in Portugal that translates to "Tell me who you hang out with, and I'll know who you are!". It's all about who I have in my life today that has called upon me to act differently.

Think about this: if you are constantly spending time with narcissistic people, your survival instinct will eventually kick in. You'll become aware that if you don't start standing up for yourself, the other person will consume you. Being around selfish, self-centred people becomes dangerous. You can wither away into nothing or find yourself becoming a narcissist yourself. I was well on my way there!

Living with a mother that was so needy and self-absorbed, my survival instinct told me that it had to be all about me; otherwise, I wouldn't survive this world. I watched her do that. My mother went through her life with a victim mentality. Making people feel sorry for her was how she took energy from others.

Luckily for me, my father and stepmother were entirely different from my mum. They were more optimistic, playful and had a can-do attitude. Life was an adventure for them, not torture. My dad suffered great losses. He was a chef and filed for bankruptcy twice. He lost his beautiful, big home, yet he never felt sorry for himself. He fought his way back every time.

Having that different perspective to observe growing up made me realise that I could choose who I wanted to become. I feel blessed to have been given other examples of how to live.

I'm sharing this with you because I want you to understand that your relationships and interactions play more of a role in your life than you could ever imagine. Relationships and friendships are breeding grounds for extreme growth. If you have a negative partner or unsupportive friends by your side, you could end up broken with nothing. But if you have a partner or friends who empower you by your side, you have the potential to achieve miracles together.

Never underestimate the power of great relationships with others. I guarantee you one of the biggest challenges you will ever face is creating, working on, building and nurturing every type of relationship you could possibly imagine, learning to become cooperative and understanding of everyone you have a relationship with. Be it your children, neighbours, boss, partner, or family;

these relationships will constantly call you to step up and connect with others.

Locking yourself away from society won't help you grow or challenge you to develop your skills. Interacting with as many different people as possible and making it work, that's what will help you grow as a person. Observing and having relationships with as many different people as possible will give you many different perspectives on what you are capable of.

It's been interesting to watch the world since the Covid-19 pandemic started. We have oscillated between social and anti-social. The lockdowns forced those afraid of their own company to look in the mirror and love themselves more. It's also caused some to become more determined to spend time together and come together as a society. The lockdowns caused a huge amount of anger to build up and the formation of little cliques or communities.

Whether we like it or not, we need each other. Now is the time to wisely select where to focus our energy to create the types of relationships we want to grow.

# CHAPTER 17

## Conclusion

This book is not an excuse for people to go and get a divorce or start cheating on their partners or force others to do as you wish. Far from it. If anything, this book is designed to reinforce integrity within your desires and needs while still respecting other people's needs. We must learn how to communicate our desires, needs and feelings to others to have others participate and share in fulfilling our desires.

We need to be loving and honest with the people around us to allow others the opportunity to engage with us (or not). There's no need to disrespect another human, control another human or take away another human's freedom simply for our benefit.

Humanity must grow up and realise that, first and foremost, we are having a relationship with ourselves, which we must learn to master. Then and only then are we be mature enough to consider a relationship with another human. Getting into a relationship when we are still getting to know ourselves becomes a distraction towards self-realisation because we then become too focused on trying to self-realise through our interactions with another person and ignore our inner self.

We must approach relationships as a healed person, not expecting another to heal us or fulfil a need that we believe we can't fulfil for ourselves. We prepare ourselves for such a commitment by being extremely honest about exactly why we want a relationship and want to get married.

In reality, many people lack the self-discipline to commit to their own career choices or healthcare, much less commit their life to another human being. When I married my husband, I definitely didn't know myself well enough. How could I have possibly been authentic enough with him if I didn't even know me? Technically my husband fell in love with someone I aspired to be, not who I really was. We are all like peacocks when we first meet someone. Well dressed, primped, preened and prancing around on our best behaviour. Master yourself first. Then consider whether you're ready to marry another.

Being able to master your relationships is how we enter higher vibrational living because, in essence, energetically, we are all one. But the only way to master our relationships is to master our individuality first. Only then can we function co-operatively as a collective without the need to suck and drain from other people.

Humans were designed to be a physical expression of Source. We were designed for expansion and growth in physical form. As a result, Source is discovering and learning about itself through us! So, if a marriage is hindering that expansion, it is stopping Source from growing and learning. Would Source willingly choose to stop its own growth process?

If you can be married and still allow for the freedom and expansion of another human while feeling free to expand and grow yourself, then, by all means, welcome marriage as an option.

# CHAPTER 18

## Frequently Asked Questions

**How do you go from always being a part of what each other does to not being involved but still being supportive?**

I'll answer this question with my favourite saying - "Your freedom ends where my freedom begins". As long as the other person's choices don't become your consequences or directly affect you, then there is little reason for you to interfere in their choices.

You can support someone without interfering—a little bit like a cheerleader. You are cheering them on but not playing the game for them. Finding this balance is one of the most challenging lessons for a parent. We spend so many years involved in our children's decisions that we become really attached to their outcomes.

As parents, we attach an underlying sense of pride and significance to what our child creates. Deep down, we understand that they are a reflection and expansion of us. Our children represent what we have created and offered to the world. So, if we are honest with ourselves, we want them to represent us accordingly. We need to become acutely aware of our personal attachments, desires, and needs in each situation to not impose our own beliefs and limitations on the other person. Remember when two birds are clinging to each other, they can't fly together.

**How do you know the difference between when someone is being caring or being controlling?**

The difference is that when someone is controlling you, it feels stifling - like your options are limited. When someone is caring for you, it feels expansive - like more options are available to you.

Let me give you a simple scenario. Imagine you want to go out with your friends and your partner believes you shouldn't go out because it's not safe. Your partner can make one of two choices. They can either say that it's unsafe for you to go out, they refuse to let you go, and they won't let you take money out of a joint account. Or they could offer options to make sure you're safe, like organising to pick you up or making sure you have enough money to arrange safe transport. The first scenario is controlling. The second is caring.

In the first scenario, the partner stops the other from doing what they want. In the second scenario, the partner offers options for the other to make sure they get what they want. There's a subtle difference, but it's one you can feel. You can feel when a partner genuinely cares for your needs. It feels different to one who cares only for their own desires. Control is always about people who want to fulfil their own needs or console their own fears.

**What stops people from doing what they want to do within a relationship?**

I think there are a few reasons why. The first thought that comes to mind is the need for approval and acceptance. Which inevitably leads to the fear of loneliness, abandonment and fear of dying alone. Then there's also the fear of change. We all desire to be loved and accepted the way we are. We will do everything we can to conform and make the other person happy.

Eventually, we realise that doing what the other person needs to feel happy isn't very self-fulfilling or gratifying to us. When we start to feel out of alignment, we consider doing something that makes *us* happy. Often it doesn't fit into another person's plan. The other person may become resistant, thinking, "Hey, she's always done what's been good for me; now she wants to change things up and do something different." All it takes is voicing the distaste for something new, and often the most flexible one will just adapt to the other.

We are a social species, and we are designed to see love and connection with other human beings. When that love and connection is threatened, especially by the beings with whom we feel safest, we become so afraid of losing that

connection that we prefer to avoid the conflict and just do

as they want.

People are more likely to go after what they want within a

relationship when they feel safe, secure, and supported. If

they know that the other person will love and accept them,

that they will support them no matter what, and that they

aren't constantly threatening to leave, one can then feel

safe to be themselves and follow their desires within a

relationship.

However, when the love and connection are conditional, a

person won't feel safe, secure or supported enough to be

themselves within a relationship. Hence, they will be

unable to do what they want without fear of ending up

alone and abandoned.

**Do you believe in divorce?**

Under the right circumstances, absolutely. If you've tried everything to make it work, if you are no longer empowering each other, stopping each other from growing, if the bad times outweigh the good times and you're no longer happy together, then absolutely.

I can only speak personally, but I don't believe in staying in an unhappy marriage. In saying that, I also don't believe in throwing in the towel too quickly either. I believe in trying different things to make it work. If necessary, take a break or time out separately first and have a cooling-off period where you don't make any permanent decisions. If both parties decide that they are better off going their own way after a cooling-off period of separation, it can be made as an amicable agreement.

**How to know when to let go or hold on?**

If you've tried everything to make it work, if you are no longer empowering each other, if you're stopping each other from growing, if the bad times outweigh the good times and you're no longer happy together, it may be time to let go. Remember, we came here for expansion and self-expression. If a marriage is not helping you expand or allowing you to express yourself, it no longer serves any purpose for both parties.

**How can I let someone live their lives without interfering, taking responsibility for them or influencing them according to my own belief systems?**

Respect comes to mind. Live and let live. When you truly love someone, you don't burden them with your own needs. They are *your* needs, not their needs. The most loving thing you can do for others is find ways to fulfil your own needs. That way, you won't feel the need to interfere in another's free will, take responsibility for their actions or even influence them. You understand that you are two individual beings.

A sense of detachment starts to occur when you respect your own free will and the free will of another. It's not a cold detachment but a detachment that brings about a sense of peace and total acceptance of another human being and yourself. Respect your individuality, and then you can finally accept another's individuality. Remember, we can't offer what we don't have within us to offer. So respect yourself first, permit yourself to be free first, then offer or teach that same sense of freedom to another.

**What's the difference between a narcissist and someone who's just very independent?**

This is a great question! They are very similar when you look at them at their most basic, superficial level.

Let's look at the dictionary definitions first. A narcissist is a person who has an excessive interest in or admiration of themselves. Independence means being free from outside control, not depending on another, not being subject to another's authority.

Someone who is highly independent, and a narcissist may appear very self-centred, self-absorbed or selfish. However, when you dig deeper and get to know them better, you notice significant differences.

An independent person is self-sufficient. They have little desire to take from another. In fact, they pride themselves on never needing others to have their needs met. In comparison, a narcissist can be very dependent on others and not care whose toes they have to step on to meet their needs. Furthermore, an independent person still has a high level of empathy and compassion towards the needs of others, even if they don't choose to engage in the drama of others. However, a narcissist has very little to no compassion for others. Their emotions only go as far as their own little world perspective. If they show any care for another person's emotions, it's either for manipulation or because it will somehow serve their own needs in the long run.

A narcissist also has a constant sense of shift in identity. They will identify with whoever gives them the most energy and attention. They can be a draining force on the people around them. When people get fed up with them, they will find someone new to feed off.

Someone independent has a sense of confidence and security within themselves. They care little about what others think of them and are quite happy to set a trend of their own and dance to the beat of their own drum.

A narcissist needs other people or external material things to keep them from feeling a sense of emptiness or boredom. They often look like they need someone to hold their hand through everything constantly. Whereas an independent person is happy to try new things, get creative, innovative, adventure and explore, even if they have to do it independently. An independent person is happy in their own company.

Lastly, someone independent is more likely to create deeper and more meaningful relationships because they have taken the time to get to know themselves well. They aren't reliant on other people's opinions of them to form a role or character in the world. A narcissist is likely to create a superficial persona based on who they spend time with. They never desire to look deeper within to find out who they are because they hadn't liked what they saw when they had done this in the past.

Sometimes it can even be conditioning of their upbringing. Maybe they were taught that what they were wasn't okay. In this case, it might be easier for them to switch off from any form of responsibility for themselves so they can't fail.

Either way, it's important to recognise the difference as you get to know them better. I highly recommend getting into relationships with people who have a strong sense of self-confidence and independence. I do not recommend getting into a relationship with a narcissist.

For more information on narcissists, check out my first book, *21st Century Relationships*, where I extensively discuss negative souls.

## Do you think we will see more polyamory? What do you have to say about throuples?

I put both these questions together because I feel the answer will be the same for both. As humanity grows in its acceptance of others' freedom, I think we will start to see more open relationships. It will take humanity a little while to develop and master the emotions necessary for this to become an acceptable norm for society. But yes, I believe we are headed towards more relationships like this, or at least acceptance rather than fear of these different types of relationships.

**Can you give some information about intimacy, sex, and the differences in expectations, needs, and wants?**

This is a big topic because we aren't only talking about gender differences but also particular desires for different types of couples. I wouldn't be able to comment on all due to a lack of experience. I imagine a woman in a gay relationship would desire and need something totally different from a heterosexual female. That's without even going into throuples, pansexual, transgender and polyamorous relationships etc. As you can imagine, each circumstance would be unique in itself.

Even within a heterosexual relationship, the differences in expectations, needs and wants are entirely different from one relationship to the next. I have personally found that some things that weren't acceptable within some of my relationships were acceptable in others. It's a matter of what's comfortable for both parties involved.

I believe that the most important trait to have when it comes to intimacy and sex is the ability to be open and accepting towards the other person and being open and accepting of your own desires. Creating an open and safe space for each other to express themselves without fear of judgment or one consistently dominating the direction of the intimacy is essential. It has to be like a dance when one steps forward, the other steps back and vice versa. When two partners are in sync, intimacy looks and feels harmonious. Most importantly, both parties come out of it feeling fulfilled.

So many couples go into sex believing that they have to put on a great show for the other! Women have to act like porn stars, and men can become engrossed in trying to give her that orgasm. What's happening is that no one is actually present with their own feelings.

People are too busy during sex trying to make it look good or feel good for the other. However, what often turns partners on is when someone fully surrenders to their desires and needs within sex and intimacy. When inhibitions are lowered, the person is fully present within their sensations.

Never approach sex for the sake of satisfying the other person. Have sex and intimacy because you want to experience it, and it will be a completely different experience.

**How soon after dating should a couple consider having sex? And how often should married couples have sex?**

I love answering questions like these because it allows me to wear different hats or answer them from different perspectives.

From a Counsellor's perspective, the correct answer would be only when the time feels right for both parties. Don't do anything if it doesn't feel right for you. But I'm inclined to add a little more to this answer.

Let's consider for a moment that sex is a homerun. Yes, I am comparing this to baseball. Now, there are technically lots of bases in between. There's the dating, going out for dinner, a movie, eventually a kiss, some foreplay, then hopefully, ultimately, there's a home run. While dating, you can clearly see this happening. It's an unusual custom to meet someone and instantly have sex with them there on the spot.

The problem is when people get married, most often, one partner will start to believe that a home run is a given. There's no longer any need to pitch a ball, hit the ball, chase after the ball. In essence, there is no longer any need to date or go out for dinner. To kiss or engage in foreplay before the home run. And that's where problems start to arise. I realise that I'm generalising, but it's most often the man who goes to bed expecting a home run without doing anything to earn that home run. In my personal opinion, this leads to a lack of appreciation for the home run. It creates a lack of respect for the earning of that home run. This can create resentment and a lack of emotional connection for the woman where she feels unworthy of more. So, she begins to cut him off at first base, yelling, "YOU'RE OUTTA HERE!" the minute he starts limbering up.

Both parties become disconnected entirely and discontented within this situation. Eventually, no one gets a home run! If only couples started viewing home runs as something they earned their way towards, the same way they did when they first picked up the bat.

A problem occasionally occurs when they score a home run too quickly on the first date. Then the man always expects that a home run will be easy and quick to achieve without putting any effort in. The woman then wonders why he's always expecting home runs to be quick and easy. He never even had to work for it! Home runs on demand!

Will this lead to a fulfilling sex life? I don't imagine it will. Will this be the couple that continues to have regular sex? No! Will the one that's getting their needs met ask for more sex? Of course. Will the one that's not getting their needs met ask for more sex? Of course not.

I'm sure there will be some out there who will say it's not fair that one should have to earn sex. Sure. Just like one shouldn't have to give it too. Even if you were to hire a lady of the night, you would still have had to earn that money you're going to pay her. It's just that earning it with a wife would mean being less lazy and emotionally earning it instead.

In conclusion, have sex when both parties feel as though it's right for both of them, and continue to have sex when both parties feel as though it's right for both! Just because it's a long-term relationship doesn't make having sex a given. The rules of the game shouldn't change, only the players.

**I seem too often get caught up in the Matrix and robotic thinking. It's always so hard to break old patterns, especially when attracting the same types of partners over and over again. How can I break out of the Matrix?**

Have you ever had an awakening experience and then forgotten it soon after? How about watching a full disclosure documentary and forgetting most of the information the day after? A week later, you remember almost none of it.

We are living within a collective energy field. Some call it the Matrix or the subconscious collective mind. I call it our 4th Dimension. It's the part of us that needs to keep us in predictable robotic patterns. This part of us is built for comfort, not growth.

When we have an awakening or experience that gets us out of our regular, predictable patterns, there's a risk we might do something different and break away from the normal patterns. If you make a change, you are essentially leaving the system or changing the program!

Could you imagine if there was no president one day and the Government said, "We aren't doing anything anymore. We will no longer take responsibility for this country—each to their own. Do whatever you want. It's survival of the fittest, good luck!" There would be so much confusion without any rules. Imagine the chaos!

The Matrix wants you to forget anything new! If it keeps you dumbed down, you won't cause any problems. You could threaten the survival of the collective system if too many of you go off course. Like if a cell in your gut now wanted to become a heart cell. The Matrix system will see it as a virus or a cell gone rogue.

When we become forgetful, we are heavily stuck within the Matrix and struggle to see other perspectives. The deeper we are ingrained in the Matrix, the more forgetful and robotic we become. It's less necessary to have a spirit to animate our physical body. When we are stuck deep within the Matrix, our Soul spends less time in our body. We become an organic vehicle on autopilot like an aeroplane or a self-driving Tesla; no one needs to be behind the wheel. You only need to be present when they need to change the direction or course of action.

I'm hoping you understand all the metaphors that I'm using. When you gain new knowledge, awareness or perspective, don't stir up too much dust within the Matrix! Stay off the radar of the collective consciousness; otherwise, they will pull out all the creative ways they can find to put you back on course.

You want your newfound awareness to go unnoticed by the system that controls you. Make changes slowly and consistently not to alarm too many people. Otherwise, expect resistance to come at you in full force to the point where you will forget everything you were trying to do. It will feel like you're constantly starting back at square one or like you're stuck in the constant process of change. It will feel like continuous self-sabotage.

Keep your energy to yourself, don't tell too many people about what you are doing; you're less likely to be targeted by the Matrix. You're less likely to attract constant self-sabotage. I have a great video on my Patreon page that explains what kinds of self-sabotage you can expect when trying to create changes. It's called Phases of Change, and you can watch it here www.patreon.com/posts/self-sabotage-of-49527396

Once you've made some changes and have been consistent with those changes, the Matrix then begins to adapt to the new you. Consider it as an upgrade within the system. It's beautiful to watch, and I discuss deeply within my Realignments.

## Have you read my other books?

How Do I Know When I'm Ready to Have Kids?

The Spiritual Awakening of a Spray Tanner

Evolve Your Emotions, Evolve Through the Dimensions

21st Century Relationships (Book 1)

Available for purchase at

www.carlasavannah.com.au

www.ingramcontent.com/pod-product-compliance
Lightning Source LLC
Chambersburg PA
CBHW072133020426
42334CB00018B/1784